HOW TO MEASURE
A RELATIONSHIP

A PRACTICAL APPROACH
TO DYADIC INTERVENTIONS

by

BARBARA STROUD

ISBN: **147934348X**
ISBN 13: **9781479343485**
Library of Congress Control Number: **2012917722**
CreateSpace Independent Publishing Platform
North Charleston, South Carolina

Dedication

This book is dedicated to my amazing daughter, Kimbal.
Every day she teaches me something new about the miracle of development.
Children can teach us so much, if we will only watch and listen.

Acknowledgement

This book would not have been possible without the support, guidance, and nurturance from some very important people:

Elizabeth Bassel

Esther Chon

Kim-Lan Dovan

Myisha Driver

Amanda Ison

Karlee Kirkpatrick

Patricia Powell

Table of Contents

Introduction

For the past twenty years, I have been working in publicly funded community mental health programs. Within these systems, I have developed programs for children up to five years old (the "birth-to-five" population) and their families, provided ongoing trainings to support over five thousand professionals, and offered the guidance of reflective supervision to numerous clinicians. The ongoing struggle I have observed professionals experiencing is the translation of a relationship-based service model from the "Identified Patient" documentation structure of publicly funding programs. I have come to recognize the need to write a book designed to specifically support mental health practitioners using public dollars with the knowledge, skills, and strategies to address this ongoing conundrum. How does one address a relationship-based intervention (the square peg) that will support the individual functioning and mental health outcomes of the child and the caregiver within the context of an individual service delivery model (the round hole)? My aim is to answer this question.

A significant point of caution is offered here: This book is not intended to substitute for high-quality training, ongoing reflective supervision, participation in ongoing study groups, or other professional development activities focused on building a strong skill set in the fundamental knowledge necessary to support the birth-to-five clinical population. Practitioners committed to gaining professional skills in the infant mental health field should look to their individual states for training competencies in infant mental health. For example, in the State of California, the Center for Infant-Family and Early Childhood Mental Health (http://cacenter-ecmh.org/) offers endorsement for qualified "infant-family and early childhood mental health" professionals and also training guidelines for professionals interested in greater knowledge. The contents of this book will only be advanced by continued training in the field of infant mental health. The necessary training domains include brain development and biological factors in development, typical developmental milestones within the birth-to-five population, family dynamics, relationship-based intervention models, assessment and diagnosis, attachment theory, and influences on parenting (http://cacenter-ecmh.org/professional-development/training-guidelines-and-personnel-competencies). This list is by no means exhaustive. As with the entire book, it is intended to be part of a larger learning process and a stepping stone towards building applied skills to support an active workforce.

What are the goals or outcome we hope for this book? The primary goal of this text is to support a current workforce of practitioners new to birth-to-five mental health service delivery. The author seeks the following outcomes:

1. Practitioners will increase their knowledge about the definition of medical necessity in birth-to-five children as well as what constitutes improvement in describing medical necessity for documentation purposes.

2. Practitioners will be able to translate observable behaviors into measurable symptoms and use these symptoms to create targeted treatment goals.

3. Practitioners will be able to use the symptoms observed to create interventions embedded in a developmental and relational understanding of the symptoms from a perspective that considers environmental stressors and issues of diversity.

4. Practitioners will be able to use observed symptoms to create interventions designed to improve the overall functioning of the relationship dyad and thus enhance overall outcomes for the child.

5. Practitioners will build their skills at developing goals which target the underlying cause of a problem behavior.

• • •

HOW TO USE THIS BOOK

This text is designed to support the clinician new to working with clients birth-to-five years of age. The goal is to prepare practitioners with the necessary skills to accurately document significant clinical observations from a developmental perspective and to define relationship-based goals and interventions that support social-emotional success and overall mental wellness in children and their caregivers.

First, we will look at symptoms and build a deeper understanding of these observed behaviors as a window into the relationship dynamic between caregiver and child. As is always the case in working with infants and toddlers, all observed behavior and dyadic interactions need to be interpreted from a developmental perspective. As we move through the text, the author will provide suggested goals to address such behaviors/symptoms from a dyadic perspective and an understanding of the developmental agenda of the child. Lastly, sample interventions will be offered that not only address current symptoms, but also connect symptom reduction to the developmental or relationship-based cause of the problem behavior. This text is intended to support, not replace, good clinical skills and build on the emerging knowledge of professionals new to the birth-to-five clinical experience.

• • •

Review of Medical Necessity

Medical necessity is a requirement to draw down Medicaid funds to provide mental health interventions to families. Medical necessity explains functional impairments in both adults and children. However, the question for our purposes would be: What does this level of impairment look like in children up to the age of five?

It is well known that our clinical training programs are highly influenced by adult models of pathology and psychotherapy. In fact, the field of child mental health can be estimated to be nearly eighty-five years old with early beginnings in the late 1920s in the writings of Melanie Klein (Klein, 1932) and Anna Freud (Freud, 1946). The infant mental health field is estimated to be approximately thirty-seven years old. Birth of the infant mental health field is often attributed to the 1975 Fraiberg publication *Ghosts in the Nursery: A Psychoanalytic Approach to the Problems of Impaired Infant-Mother Relationships*.

Guidelines for medical necessity derived from the early traditions of Klein and Freud, parallel the standard of scaling down of adult clinical theories to create clinical models for children. Medical necessity in an adult can be defined as the incapacity to manage daily functions, including successful interaction with the environment and social networks (such as going to work, having positive family relationships, maintaining proper hygiene, and self-care). For children, therapists often look to academic and social success in school, positive peer relationships, and amicable family interactions as evidence of functional success.

Keeping it Simple:

Definition of Medical Necessity

Medical necessity for intervention can be explained as the failure in one's interpersonal interactions or activities. An individual is unable to function appropriately by relating in a socially and culturally acceptable manner in their community.

Add to this the understanding that individuals play an interactive role in their environment thus explaining how functional capacity is influenced by interpersonal relationships (which are affected by intrapersonal processes). As a result, the quality of a person's relationships (with caregivers, peers, or professionals) can lead to successful or less than optimal outcomes.

The Psychological Tasks of Childhood

In the field of infant mental health, we often take a bottom-up approach (Lillas & Turnbull, 2009) and seek to weave optimal developmental outcomes with healthy social-emotional influences to build up a child. Thus, rather than taking an approach from a scaled-down adult model, we start developmentally with what all children need to be successful in interpersonal interactions and in life. From this perspective, we answer the question: What are the psychological tasks or required skills young children must achieve for social-emotional success? The psychological tasks of infants and preschoolers are listed here:

1. To develop a strong secure attachment bond

2. To learn to modulate external sensory input

3. To learn to manage their internal affective states

4. To effectively communicate and get their needs met

5. To effectively adapt to their changing world

These psychological tasks are required and necessary for social-emotional success (i.e., mental wellness). As models of resilience continue to grow favor in public mental health care, providers must be knowledgeable in regards to the skills very young children need to master for success later in life. One such skill, building a strong attachment relationship, is a significant protective factor for children (Werner & Smith, 1992). Young children are biologically driven to engage in attachment behaviors to create the nexus for their caregivers to fall madly in love with them and protect them from harm (Bowlby, 1958, 1980). Children that feel strongly connected to a loving and caring adult attachment figure demonstrate greater resilience

7

against adversity than children lacking this type of relationship (Alink, Cicchetti, Kim, & Rogosch, 2009; Schore, 2001). A strong, early attachment will also positively impact a child's self-esteem and feelings of self-worth. Caregiver relationships are the primary architects of a child's internal model for attachment (Ainsworth, 1979).

Significant within the first few months of life is the infant's capacity to modulate sensory input, to stay calm and alert in the face of new and sometimes distressing external stimulation. Newborns are faced with an ongoing assault of new external sensory information (e.g., bright lights, loud noises, and the contrast in temperature when going into and out of the bath). All these sensory experiences must be integrated and organized by the brain of the infant over time. In optimal situations, the child habituates (or grows accustomed) to new sensory information and expands his window of alert processing (Brazelton, 1992). Multiple factors support this skill, including a strong neurological constitution, consistent caregiving responses, and the absence of significant sensory integration abnormalities in the child. Without the developed capacity to habituate to new sensory information, children and adults would be continually distracted and distressed by ongoing sensory information (e.g., the sound of a siren passing by, the rumble on the ground initiated by a large truck passing by, or the glare of the sunlight through the windowpane). Adults and children learn over time to accommodate new sensory information without incident. This allows for attention and engagement in relationships (one cannot focus or communicate if upset by sensory input). Modulating sensory experiences is one aspect of self-regulation. The capacity to regulate can be defined as the skill to organize and integrate both internal and external input in a manner that allows the child to be emotionally present, ready to learn, and engage socially. Thus, the capacity to modulate sensory input supports regulation and engagement, which are necessary skills to support the ability to work, play, and be productive.

The capacity to manage internal affective states is an early activity of childhood. (Yes, babies have feelings.) What does the research literature tell us about how babies learn to identify, understand, and express feelings? Lifelong skills of affective management and emotional understanding begin in the earliest relationships with caregivers (Fonagy, Gergely, Jurist, & Target, 2004; Gergely & Watson, 1996). As caregivers engage in the activities of nurturance, they are shaping the developing understanding of emotional experiences. Young children learn how to understand emotions in part by how caregivers model their experiences. Children also learn internal skills of affect management by how their caregivers narrate or explain their affective states as well as the affective states of the child. For example, a mother might state, "Little Jessica, you look so happy, look at that smile and you are giggling and talking to Mommy. I just love it when we can share happy times together." Or on a different note, "David, Mommy is feeling very frustrated after all that traffic, but I am doing my very best to get you your dinner because I can see you are very hungry." Finally, we know that early relational experiences with nurturing responses from caregivers can shape brain development in the sub-regions that directly influence the autonomic nervous system responses (Perry, 2001; Schore, 1994; Siegel, 1999). This region of the brain is responsible for stress responses in children and adults. Furthermore, we know that developing stress responses are shaped by interactions with caregivers (Hane & Fox, 2006). The models of managing feelings that caregivers provide children in the early years often become the child's expressed template for affect regulation (Schore, 2001).

Effective communication is a necessary functional skill required throughout the life span. However, many professionals may not be fully aware of the subtle, nonverbal, and ongoing cues infants demonstrate to caregivers in order to communicate their needs. Infants who have their needs responded to in a timely and accurate manner begin to understand that they can influence others and their world in a manner that provides necessary developmental support. However, infants that do not have their needs responded to in a timely or accurate manner may internalize expectations that the world is unpredictable, that caregivers cannot meet their needs, or that they (as individuals) are powerless over their experiences. It is common for mental health professionals to see children who missed this early responsiveness to cueing, and instead use dramatic, violent, or socially inappropriate methods to seek adult responsiveness because more subtle activities have proven ineffective. Mental health professionals may also see the opposite functional response in infants or toddlers who are shut down, disengaged, or not animated. These children often miss intervention because they are seen as "easy" and do not create disruption in their environments (childcare, preschool, or home).

An important skill developed in early childhood that is necessary across the life span is the ability to adapt to change or to successfully manage life's transitions. Consider the multitude of changes in a single day that an infant or toddler experiences: sleep to wake, wet to dry to wet, from the home to the car, to the childcare provider, and so on. The young child is expected to stay self-regulated or emotionally organized and available for engagement during such transitions. The elements that support success in the face of change are:

1. A secure adult attachment relationship

2. Consistent and nurturing caregiving

3. Sensitive caregiver responses

4. Narration of the emotional world of the infant and caregiver

Young children served in the mental health system may have lacked sensitive and responsive care and may have come from chaotic or emotionally unstable environments. Such children can find transitions to be points of distress. "Good enough" caregivers work with their children to successfully move them through an ever-changing world (Thomas & Chess, 1977). On the other hand, overburdened caregivers, easily overwhelmed by the multiple demands of daily living, will need the assistance of a sensitive clinician to build up their internal resources so that they can act as the necessary objects of support, nurturance, and strength that their children will need to move successfully through transitions.

THE PSYCHOLOGICAL TASKS OF CHILDHOOD

- To develop a strong secure attachment bond

- To learn to modulate external sensory input

- To learn to manage their internal affective states

- To effectively communicate and get their needs met

- To effectively adapt to their changing world

The above tasks will naturally develop in a child with the support of an emotionally available caregiver.

TO SUPPORT THE CHILD'S PSYCHOLOGICAL DEVELOPMENT THE PARENT MUST DEMONSTRATE THE FOLLOWING TASKS:

- A secure attachment relationship

- Consistent and nurturing

- Sensitive caregiver responses

- Narration of the emotional world of the infant

Symptoms of Concern—When Do Problem Behaviors Become Clinical Symptoms?

From the lens of the practitioners working within the birth-to-five community, it is important to understand that symptoms or challenging behaviors in young children are often a signal of distress in the caregiver-child relationship. One cannot separate the social-emotional development of a child from the interpersonal and environmental conditions of the caregiver-child dyad (Kochanska, Philibert, & Barry, 2009). To understand symptoms and plan interventions, practitioners must see beyond the initial problem behavior and look to the developmental or relational cause of the behavior. This need to *look deeper* into the root of the problem will assist the practitioner in the development of goals and interventions. Common problem behaviors become symptoms when functional impairment is evident. Practitioners need to look at these behaviors using the questions provided in the *causal rubric:*

1. Is this behavior the result of a developmental delay or constitutional limitation in the child?

2. Does this behavior result from a less than optimal relationship dynamic, and serve as the child's best efforts in this system to get his/her needs met?

3. Is this behavior the byproduct of intense stress in the system or severe trauma?

4. Are the current problem behaviors at a sufficient level of disorder or distress, such that impairment in the child's functioning is evident?

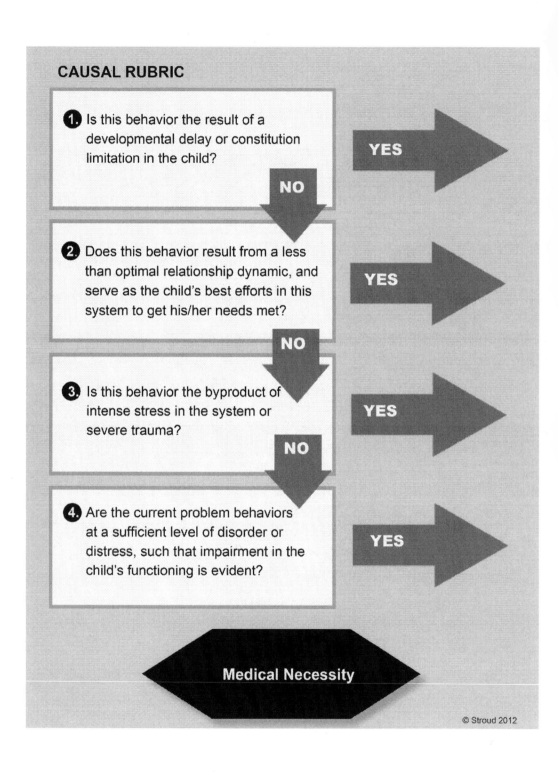

CAUSAL RUBRIC

1. Is this behavior the result of a developmental delay or constitution limitation in the child?

YES

NO

2. Does this behavior result from a less than optimal relationship dynamic, and serve as the child's best efforts in this system to get his/her needs met?

YES

NO

3. Is this behavior the byproduct of intense stress in the system or severe trauma?

YES

NO

4. Are the current problem behaviors at a sufficient level of disorder or distress, such that impairment in the child's functioning is evident?

YES

Medical Necessity

© Stroud 2012

Practitioners are warned here to be mindful that the four questions in the causal rubric are not mutually exclusive. For example, a child may both have a developmental delay (poor speech and language) and be exposed to trauma (death of a parent). While one or more foundational issues may impact the observed behavior, the important concept for practitioners is to ask these questions. Some readers may be familiar with other diagnostic triage systems that begin by ruling out trauma. As professionals, we are aware that trauma can disrupt developmental progress and influence relationship outcomes. This author has chosen to start from the internal state of the child and then move outward towards the influences of relationships and environmental factors. The perspective taken considers an approach that begins from the inside and then seeks to consider external events. It is by design that this approach serves as a parallel to the strength-based value of the infant mental health field. All readers are encouraged to begin their causal rubric with the child's current strengths and vulnerabilities, developmental age, and functional capacities. Begin by asking: What are the developmental capacities of this child, at this moment in time, as influenced by current relationships and his/her unique environmental conditions? This focuses on the influential factors that impact emotional learning. The answers to the rubric questions will assist practitioners in creating goals and interventions. We will now provide an example to put our causal rubric into practice. Considering the behavior of excessive crying in a seventeen-month-old child, a practitioner can develop the causal rubric questions in this way:

1. Is this behavior the result of a developmental delay or constitutional limitation in the child?

    a. Have physiological causes for severe pain or discomfort been ruled out?

    b. Does the child have significant sensory aversions?

    c. Does this child appear to be on track with areas of general development—motor, language, self-help, social-emotional?

2. Does this behavior result from a less then optimal relationship dynamic, and serve as the child's best efforts in this system to get his/her needs met?

   a. Does the caregiver demonstrate sensitive and attuned responses to the child's cues?

   b. Is the caregiver emotionally well regulated and able to support the ongoing development of self-regulation in the child?

   c. What is the quality of the dyad's relationship, as assessed by Axis II of ZERO TO THREE's DC: 0-3R (2005)—e.g., overinvolved, underinvolved, anxious/tense, angry/hostile?

3. Is this behavior the byproduct of intense stress in the system or severe trauma?

   a. What environmental conditions may be contributing to stress in the relationship?

   b. What is the caregiver's capacity to co-regulate the child in the face of stressful conditions?

   c. Does this family system experience ongoing stress that does not abate and thus reaches the level of trauma?

4. Are the current problem behaviors at a sufficient level of disorder or distress, such that impairment in the child's functioning is evident?

   a. In what way do you observe the problem behavior as negatively impacting the child's development, overall function, and ongoing social-emotional success?

CAUSAL RUBRIC - EXAMPLE EXCESSIVE CRYING

1. Is this behavior the result of a developmental delay or constitutional limitation in the child?

YES →
- Have physiological factors been ruled out?
- Does the child have significant sensory aversions?
- Does this child appear to be on track in areas of general development – motor, language, self-help, social –emotional?

NO ↓

2. Does this behavior result from a less than optimal relationship dynamic, and serve as the child's best efforts in this system to get his/her needs met?

YES →
- Does the caregiver demonstrate sensitive and attuned responses to the child's cues?
- Is the caregiver emotionally well-regulated and able to support the self-regulation of the child?
- What is the dyad's relationship quality as assessed by Axis II of the DC: 0-3R

NO ↓

3. Is this behavior the byproduct of intense stress in the system or severe trauma?

YES →
- What environmental conditions may be contributing to stress in the relationship?
- What is the caregiver's capacity to co- regulate the child in the face of stressful conditions?
- Does this family system experience ongoing stress that does not abate and thus reaches the level of trauma?

NO ↓

4. Are the current problem behaviors at a sufficient level of disorder or distress, such that impairment in the child's functioning is evident?

YES →
In what way do you observe the problem behavior as negatively impacting the child's development, overall function, and ongoing social-emotional success?

© Stroud 2012

17

Defining the Underlying Cause of Symptoms

The symptom checklist is designed to help the practitioner new to birth-to-five work understand the manner in which young children may express distress. The checklist is categorized by symptom or behavior and further subdivided by age. Remember that caregivers come to practitioners with behaviors of concern. Practitioners determine a symptom is present when functional impairment is the result of the behavior. This symptom checklist is provided as a resource to help the practitioner make use of the causal rubric and to begin goal development for documentation purposes.

Keeping it Simple:

Definition of a Problem Symptom

Symptoms are simply behaviors we can observe and measure. These behaviors are difficult for the caregiver, the child, or both to manage. Thus, these behaviors can negatively impact development.

---

0 to 2	3 to 5

Disruptive Behavior

- Tantrums
- Crying
- Head Banging
- Smearing Feces

- Tantrums
- Aggression towards others
- Breaking toys
- Bad Language

Emotional dysregulation or mood instability (too much affect, too little affect, or out of control affect)

UPREGULATED

- Excessive Crying
- Overwhelming Affect
- Crying, screaming, tantruming
- Poor sleeping
- Poor eating

DOWNREGULATED

- Poor or no eye contact
- Does not seek comfort from caregiver
- Does not signal when distressed
- Oversleeping

UPREGULATED

- Intensity of affect greater then parent can manage
- Intense rage, breaking objects
- Hurting self or others

DOWNREGULATED

- Lack of interest in peers for social play
- Oversleeping
- Isolative at home and school
- Limited expression of affect

Impulsivity (resulting from stress, trauma, sensory needs, or ADHD)

- Difficulty tracking
- Cannot attend to caregiver or a single object for a sustained period of time

- Poor attention
- Moves from one activity to another demonstrating little interest or sustained attention
- Impulsive responses
- Inability to focus and sustain attention in adult-child interactions
- Unable to maintain attention to toy or task for 4 to 7 minutes

© Stroud 2012

0 to 2	3 to 5

Lack of attunement or attachment to a caregiver

- Does not respond to caregiver's attempt to soothe when upset
- Does not seek comfort from adults
- Poor sleep schedule
- Caregiver repeatedly misses infant's cues
- Caregiver responds to infant's cues in a manner that is incongruent to infant's needs

- Poor attachment –does not safely explore his or her world- meets caregiver after separation with anger or indifference
- Talks to or goes with strangers
- Lack of empathy for others

Poor social relationship skills with peers

- Lack of mutual engagement with primary caregiver (Infants are not expected to engage with peers)

- Does not share with peers
- Takes toys from peers without asking
- Aggressive behavior with peers – hits, bites, kicks, pulls hair, etc.
- Calls others names
- Will not follow adult directions

Withdrawn, disconnected, isolated

- Poor eye contact
- Feeding problems
- Lack of social smile or emotional vitality
- Oversleeping
- Limited vocalization
- Slow to warm/difficult to engage

- Plays alone or not at all
- Does not engage with others
- Flat affect or limited expression of affect
- Fearful in new situations
- Does not engage caregiver when distressed

© Stroud 2012

21

Creating Goals That Support Relationships

This goal bank has been created to supplement the beginning practitioner's clinical knowledge base. Practitioners using this system should enhance the goal bank suggestions with their clinical judgment and quality supervision. The goal bank models the same layout as the symptom checklist, arranged according to the concerning symptom then subdivided by age. For each symptom, there is a set of suggested goals that are not to be considered all inclusive. The practitioner must use these goals in conjunction with the previously presented causal rubric in order to determine the best fit for a given treatment dyad or family. To determine the best fit, a practitioner should consider the influences of family culture, the caregiver's emotional capacity, the child's developmental needs, and individual differences within the self-regulation and social-emotional capacities of the child. Goals are a method for stating expected outcomes for treatment in a measurable manner. Goals should also define the skill or behavior a child is expected to master in order to mitigate the problematic symptoms.

Keeping it Simple:

Definition of a Goal

Goals should define a measurable symptom and outline the results of the intervention, which will be to increase a protective factor or to decrease a risk factor.

GOALS TO ADDRESS DISRUPTIVE BEHAVIOR

0 to 2

- Infant will decrease tantrums (screaming, hitting self, throwing self on floor) from 6 times a day to 1 time a day
- Infant will increase ability to co-regulate with the assistance of a supportive adult model from 1 time a day to 3 times a day

3 to 5

- Child will decrease incidents of aggressive actions (hitting, biting, spitting, throwing objects) towards others at school and home from 7 times a day to 4 times a day
- Child will increase feelings vocabulary and practice in session the use of expressive language to communicate feelings from 0 times to 3 times in session
- Child will seek out a caregiver, teacher, or the therapist for assistance to co-regulate distressing affect from 0 times a week to 5 times a week

GOALS TO ADDRESS MOOD INSTABILITY

0 to 2

UPREGULATED

- Infant will decrease excessive crying (2 or more hours for 3 or more times a day) from 6 days to 2 days
- Infant will increase response to co-regulation from attentive caregiver from 4 times per day to 8 times per day
- Infant will successfully cue available and responsive caregiving adult in order to seek co-regulation of affect from 3 times a day to 8 times a day
- With the aid of a structured sleep routine, infant will successfully sleep without waking in distress from 3 hour time spans at night to 5 hour time spans

DOWNREGULATED

- Infant will sustain eye contact with caregiver (using age appropriate gaze aversion) from 3 minutes to 10 minutes
- Infant will signal caregiver when in distress from 0 times a day to 5 times a day
- Infant will demonstrate age-appropriate fluctuations in mood as evident by joyful engagement, playful vocalization, and brief periods of disengagement to re-organize and return to an interaction, from 2 times a day to 8 times a day

3 to 5

UPREGULATED

- Child will demonstrate age-appropriate mood as evidenced by demonstrations of joint attention (reciprocal play) with caregiver from 2 minutes to 10 minutes
- Child will successfully demonstrate age-appropriate mood as evidenced by the ability to seek out a caregiver for nurturance when upregulated or emotionally overwhelmed from 2 times a day to 6 times a day
- Child will decrease the throwing of objects (and/or) hitting of others from 15 times a day to 8 times a day
- Child will increase use of feeling words to express affective states to supportive caregivers from 0 times a day to 5 times a day

DOWNREGULATED

- Child will increase joyful reciprocal play with caregiver from 0 times a day to 3 times a day
- Child will express shared joy in playful engagement activities with peers or siblings from 0 times a day to 3 times a day
- Child will make use of feeling cards to express his/her affective experience within the classroom setting from 0 times a day to 3 times a day
- Child will build a feelings vocabulary in clinical session and make use of 1 new feeling word in interactions with family and peers from 0 times a week to 6 times a week

© Stroud 2012

GOALS TO ADDRESS IMPULSIVE BEHAVIORS

0 to 2

- Infant will demonstrated engagement and attention to caregiver by tracking caregiver in familiar and novel settings from 0 times to 3 times a day
- Increase infant's capacity for joint attention from 3 minutes to 12 minutes from 2 times a day to 8 times a day

3 to 5

- Child will increase ability to sustain attention in an age-appropriate task during play from 2 minutes to 10 minutes
- Child will demonstrate joint attention with a caregiving adult from 4 minutes to 15 minutes
- Child will demonstrate sustained shared attention with peers and toys from 5 minutes to 15 minutes
- Child will decrease out of seat behaviors from 8 times a day to 3 times a day

GOALS TO ADDRESS LACK OF ATTUNEMENT TO CAREGIVER

0 to 2

- Infant will successfully cue caregiver and be met with sensitive responses from 3 times a day to 9 times a day
- Infant will demonstrate the ability to calm in response to interventions from caregiver from 0 times a day to 7 times a day
- Infant will socially reference caregiver in new or distressing environments from 0 time a week to 5 times a week
- With support from caregiver, toddler will safely explore new environments from 0 times to 4 times a week
- Infant will decrease excessive crying from 4 times a day of 3 or more hours to 0 times a day of 3 or more hours

3 to 5

- Child will successfully transition from caregiver to childcare environment without excessive crying from 2 times a week to 5 times a week
- Child will greet caregiver with joy or actively seek caregiver to soothe distress following a period of separation from 2 times a week to 5 times a week
- Child will use feeling words to articulate emotional states such as happy, sad, mad, or scared, from 0 times a week to 6 times a week
- Child will decrease wondering away from parent in community settings from 5 times a week to 0 times a week
- Child will demonstrate the ability to predict the feeling states of peers and seek adult support to help peers in distress from 0 times a week to 2 times a week

GOALS TO ADDRESS POOR SOCIAL RELATIONSHIP SKILLS WITH PEERS

0 to 2

- Toddler will demonstrate sustained engagement with caregiver and interactions of shared joy from 1 time a day to 4 times a day
- Toddler will demonstrate the ability to successfully participate in parallel play without hitting peers or fighting over toys from 2 times a day to 4 times a day
- Toddler will decrease striking peers with toys from 5 times a day to 0 times a day

3 to 5

- Child will successfully engage in same age peer play without demonstrations of physical violence towards peers from 2 times a day to 6 times a day
- Child will sustain joint attention to one adult and 2 peers without, hitting, biting, or throwing objects, from 1 time a day to 4 times a day
- Child will decrease incidents of (hitting, biting, yelling, pulling hair, or taking toys.) for 7 times a day to 3 times a day
- Child will follow adult directions on the 2nd request from 0 times a day to 3 times a day

GOALS TO ADDRESS WITHDRAWN, DISCONNECTED, ISOLATED

0 to 2

- Infant will increase eye contact with caregiver from 2 minutes to 6 minutes, when child is in an alert state
- Infant will decrease reflux (spitting up of meals) with co-regulation support from caregiver from 7 times a day to 2 times a day
- Infant will increase spontaneous vocalizations from 3 times a day to 10 times a day
- Infant will respond to caregiver or sibling's gaze with a social smile and/or verbal cue from 2 times a day to 8 times a day

3 to 5

- Child will increase age-appropriate play interactions with peers from 0 times a day to 3 times a day
- Child will participate in shared attention and playful activities with caregiver for 10 minute intervals from 0 times a week to 5 times a week
- Child will demonstrate joyful expressions of laughter, smiles, and excited vocalizations while engaging with peers, family members, or therapist from 1 time a day to 5 times a day
- Child will successfully seek support and co-regulation from caregiving adults in the face of novel or fearful stimuli from 0 times a day to 3 times a day

© Stroud 2012

Building Interventions to Support Relationships

There are multiple activities in which a mental health practitioner can engage to provide therapeutic support to a young child and caregivers. Interventions should be thoughtfully designed not only to achieve the desired goal of symptom abatement, but to treat the underlying cause of the challenging behavior. Practitioners' professional scope of practice allows them to analyze the interplay of the complexity of causal factors for pathology, the child's developmental agenda, and the family's culture and related parenting expectations, thereby creating interventions from a defined theoretical understanding of the underlying causes for the problematic behavior. In this text, we have introduced the reader to a causal rubric strategy designed to help organize clinical observations to create structured goals. We will now link this strategy to the development of treatment interventions. At the point of creating interventions the fourth rubric question regarding medical necessity should be satisfied and is therefore omitted here. The reader is reminded of our primary rubric questions for causal understanding:

1. Is this behavior the result of a developmental delay or constitutional limitation in the child? (In other words, can the cause of the problem be understood as rooted in the state of the child's character?)

2. Does this behavior result from a less than optimal relationship dynamic, and serve as the child's best efforts in this system to get his/her needs met? (In other words, can the cause of the problematic behavior be best understood as resulting from the interpersonal dynamics of the caregiver-child relationship?)

3. Is this behavior the byproduct of intense stress in the system or severe trauma? (In other words, can the primary reason for the developmental issue be linked to an environmental cause that limits success for the dyad?)

The first question points us to the child's constitution- or state-dependent causes for behavioral problems, while the second question defines problems influenced by issues in the relationship. Finally, the third question describes behaviors resulting primarily from environmental causes. Often symptoms are the result of an interaction of factors (e.g., state-dependent issues that affect relationship factors or environmental events that influence the child's specific state issue). The intervention grid offers interventions from these three causal perspectives as correlated with problem symptoms. This intervention grid provides a structure to enable practitioners to begin to contemplate the best interventions from a deeper understanding of the underlying cause(s) of the problematic behavior.

The intervention grid provides suggested interventions rather than an exhaustive list of treatment approaches. The new practitioner should note how the same target behavior is approached differently according to the causal nature of the symptom—there are interventions that target improvement in the child's internal capacity, interventions designed to build coherence in the dyad, and interventions focused more on environmental factors to support optimal developmental outcomes. As we have cautioned throughout the text, these interventions are offered as a helpful guide to novice practitioners as their skills develop. Always consult with your immediate supervisor to ensure that suggested interventions are acceptable under your specific funding guidelines.

CAUSAL RUBRIC - TO SUPPORT INTERVENTIONS

1. Is this behavior the result of a developmental delay or constitutional limitation in the child?

- Have physiological factors been ruled out?
- Does the child have significant sensory aversions?
- Does this child appear to be on track in areas of general development – motor, language, self-help, social –emotional?

If the answers to Causal Question #1 are yes - Consider a State *Dependent Intervention*

2. Does this behavior result from a less than optimal relationship dynamic, and serve as the child's best efforts in this system to get his/her needs met?

- Does the caregiver demonstrate sensitive and attuned responses to the child's cues?
- Is the caregiver emotionally well-regulated and able to support the self-regulation of the child?
- What is the dyad's relationship quality as assessed by Axis II of the DC: 0-3R?

If the answers to Causal Question # 2 are yes - Consider a *Relationship Dependent Intervention*

3. Is this behavior the byproduct of intense stress in the system or severe trauma?

- What environmental conditions may be contributing to stress in the relationship?
- What is the caregiver's capacity to co- regulate the child in the face of stressful conditions?
- Does this family system experience ongoing stress that does not abate and thus reaches the level of trauma?

If the answers to Causal Question # 3 are yes - Consider an *Environment Dependent Intervention*

© Stroud 2012

SYMPTOM	STATE DEPENDENT *EX: CHILD WITH A DEVELOPMENTAL DELAY*	RELATIONSHIP DEPENDENT *EX: INFANT WITH A DEPRESSED MOTHER*	ENVIRONMENT DEPENDENT *EX: CHILD IN A HOME WITH DOMESTIC VIOLENCE*
Disruptive Behavior	• Caregiver will support child's capacity to regulate when faced with overwhelming affective states, through use of sensory strategies, emotion narration and co-regulation	• Caregiver will practice self-regulation and maintain a calm state in the face of child's aggressive outbursts • When child becomes aggressive caregiver will remain calm and use a 3 step supportive strategy 1) regulate child 2) narrate feelings & 3) redirect to safe behavior	• Caregiver will increase structure through use of daily routines, picture schedules, or scripted stories when appropriate to support child's ability to self-regulate • Therapist will introduce a feelings thermometer* and teach child to self-monitor his/her feelings states – caregiver will respond to child's self-reported affective experiences by providing increased emotional support as child indicates increased emotional distress
Mood instability	• Caregivers, teachers, and therapist will provide child with words, picture cards, and sign language to communicate feeling states and reflect back feeling states to the child • Child will practice self-regulatory techniques with caregiver such as deep breathing, sensory supports, use of angry bottle* or paper tearing	• Caregivers will offer timely and nurturing responses to child's emotional needs which include validation of feeling and co-regulation to increase capacity for self-regulation • Caregiver will establish and maintain daily opportunities for child-directed play to support social-emotional development and build increased moments of joy within the dyad	• Caregiver will post feelings charts in the home and narrate his/her own feeling states to the child during the day (e.g. "Daddy is so frustrated! Can you help me take 3 deep breaths?" "Mommy is crying because she is feeling sad and everyone feels sad sometimes.") • Therapist will assist the caregiver in creating an Angry Center* in the home to assist child in discharging negative affect • Therapist will assist the caregiver in creating a Relaxation Center* in the home to assist the child in building self-comforting strategies
Impulsive responses	• Therapist, caregiver and child will play stop motion games such as slow motion tag* or the freeze games* in order to teach skills to slow impulsive responses • With the support of caregiver and teacher, child will practice counting to 3 prior to asking a question of an adult	• Caregiver will prepare child for new activities by explaining upcoming daily events (e.g. trip to the grocery store or visit to a friend's home), caregiver will outline the expected behavior for the event and provide child with age-appropriate games or tasks if child becomes distracted	• Caregiver will post a visual schedule of the morning route for child to self-monitor • Teacher and caregiver will post reminder signs (STOP-LOOK-LISTEN) to remind the child to slow impulsive responses, look to others for direction, listen to adults for feedback

© Stroud 2012

* see Glossary of terms for definitions of these activities

SYMPTOM	STATE DEPENDENT	RELATIONSHIP DEPENDENT	ENVIRONMENT DEPENDENT
	EX: CHILD WITH A DEVELOPMENTAL DELAY	*EX: INFANT WITH A DEPRESSED MOTHER*	*EX: CHILD IN A HOME WITH DOMESTIC VIOLENCE*
Poor attunement	• Caregiver will increase child's alert processing window by attending to moments of focused attention with mirroring of child's affect • Caregiver will offer play activities that increase visual tracking and seek to create greater opportunities for eye contact	• Caregiver will increase ability to notice and respond to cues using touch, tone of voice, and proximity • Therapist will coach caregiver in mirroring of vocalizations of child to support the attachment bond	• Therapist will assist caregiver in creating opportunities during the day for structured play-such as: sensory games, peak-a-boo, tickle time, or any interactions that increase social engagement
Social Skills w/ Peers	• Therapist will support child in building skills to read the social cues of others. • Child will make use of a squeeze ball when agitated and use squeeze ball to decrease name-calling, hitting others, or grabbing toys from peers	• Therapist will build caregiver's skills to narrate the events of the child's experience during a peer interaction (e.g. "Johnny do you want to play with Suzy? Ask Suzy if she likes to play ball. Are you shy? Mommy can help you.") • Caregiver, teacher, and therapist will build child's understanding of cause and effect as related to peer interactions. (e.g. "Nancy will not want to play with you if you take her toy without asking. That is such nice sharing; sharing is how you show others you care.")	• Caregiver will post rules for interpersonal behavior in the home (we do not hit and use nice words with others) • Caregiver will plan opportunities for peer play interactions, provide supervision, and offer ongoing narration as child builds his/her skill set
Withdrawn or Disconnected	• Caregiver will respond to child's social cues with high animation and heightened affective expression • Therapist and caregiver will mirror exaggerated affect to increase child's emotional responsiveness to social cues	• Caregiver will increase frequency and intensity of response to child's engagement cues through touch, tone of voice, and proximity • Caregiver will establish and maintain daily opportunities for child-directed play to support social-emotional development and build increased moments of joy within the dyad	• Caregiver will take child to the park and increase opportunities for peer-to-peer engagement • Caregiver will connect child to age-appropriate and affordable recreational activity (soccer, art class, dance, etc.)

© Stroud 2012

* see Glossary of terms for definitions of these activities

Treatment Planning Considerations

In order to build a well-rounded treatment plan, practitioners may want to start with what is working well. When observing the dyad, look for where success is evident in the relationship. What are the strengths of the caregiver and the strengths of the child? Knowing the developmental capacities of each member of the dyad as well as their observable strengths gives the practitioner a starting point for intervention. Use what caregivers know how to do to scaffold new skills and abilities.

At this time, we will list common domains that produce early relationship distress in caregiver-child dyads. From an understanding of these domains will come treatment suggestions. Again, caution: These suggestions are meant only to support the reader's learning.

When impairment in the relationship interaction is the function of delays in the child's social-emotional development, the treatment plan should assist the caregiver in moving the child through his or her age-appropriate social-emotional milestones. Strategies can include:

1. Using Greenspan's (2007) social-emotional milestones to assess and improve expressed social-emotional skills

2. Using play to scaffold skill building within the social-emotional domain

3. Educating the caregiver on the importance of social-emotional development as it relates to cognition and learning

When the dyad's optimal functioning is hampered due to disruptions in the attachment system, the treatment may need to focus on strengthening the attachment relationship between the caregiver and the child. Strategies can include:

1. Working to increase the caregiver's responsiveness

2. Supporting the caregiver's ability to accurately read the infant's cues

3. Assisting the caregiver in creating a balanced, affective tone when responding to the needs of the child

4. Increasing back-and-forth nurturing responses

5. Increasing loving and joyful interactions within the dyad

6. Helping to organize a daily routine that creates predictability for the caregiver

At times, the developmental success of the child is hampered by the limitations of the caregiver's stress level, mental health issues, or substance recovery issues. For cases in which the caregiver's skills are compromised, treatment can focus on building up the caregiver's parenting competence and confidence. Strategies can include:

1. Applying strength-based approaches with the caregiver

2. Engaging in activities that develop parenting skills

3. Exploring historical parenting experiences

4. Increasing attuned responses that match the child's emotional needs

5. Building the caregiver's ability to reflect the child's experience

6. Elongating moments of joy within the dyad

Finally, stressful environmental conditions such as domestic violence, chronic stress, poverty, social deprivation, or loss can impede optimal developmental outcomes for a child. When these concerns are significant, practitioners should incorporate strategies to decrease external stress, increase consistency in the environment, and connect families to networks of support. Strategies can include:

1. Increasing family routines and daily rituals

2. Connecting families to natural supports

3. Increasing affect management strategies for all family members

Protective Factors

At any point in the practitioner's relationship with a family system, an emphasis on increasing protective factors can be valuable. Protective factors serve to mitigate risk factors and strengthen internal or external support systems. Internal skills that can serve as protective factors include self-regulation, secure attachment connections, the capacity for empathetic understanding, adequate physical health, and appropriate social-emotional development. External protective factors can include high-quality preschool or childcare, emotional and physical safety in the home, access to age-appropriate recreation or leisure activities, social support systems (e.g., family, friends, clubs, or groups), and involvement in faith-based or cultural communities of support. Considering protective factors in treatment planning creates links to resources and community networks that can sustain mental wellness and live long beyond the prescribed treatment intervention period.

Always remember a practitioner's primary intervention tool is the relationship. To keep their toolboxes well equipped, practitioners should participate in reflective supervision for the benefit of themselves and the children and families they serve. Young children need caregivers to support their optimal development. Caregivers often need professionals to offer support and guidance as they seek to meet the emotional needs of their children. Practitioners need supportive and emotionally available supervisors to assist them in keeping focused on the optimal outcomes for each family, as aligned with the family's culture and personal values. The greatest gift we can give children and families is self-sufficiency to create their own success.

Good luck on your professional journey.

Glossary

Angry Bottle –

An angry bottle can be made at home or in therapy with an empty plastic drinking bottle of six to eight ounces. In the bottle, add water (until the bottle is full), red food coloring, and a small amount of dish soap. Then secure the top of the bottle with a strong adhesive. The angry bottle can be shaken at a time of distress to assist a child in calming down.

Angry Center –

An angry center can be created at home or school to support the child's ability to self-regulate or self-calm when distressed. In an angry center, activities that support the child's self-regulation are available for use at the child's request or at the adult's suggestion. Items you may wish to include an angry bottle, play dough for smashing, paper for scribbling or tearing, stuffed animals for hugging or safely throwing, and soft balls for safely throwing or squeezing.

Feelings Thermometer –

A feelings thermometer can be made or found online to download. With the highest indicator symbolizing maximum distress or anger, and the lowest threshold indicating relaxed and alert states, this template allows children capable of symbolic language to communicate their level of distress. Teachers, caregivers, or therapists can cue a child to use the thermometer to identify their level of distress and monitor their internal states.

Freeze Games-

Freeze games are any stop/action games. In such an activity, the therapist, teacher, or caregiver can use music or a bell to signal the stopping of an action. Children can play a freeze dance game (i.e., when the music stops, freeze) or a freeze tag game, (i.e., when the teacher says "freeze," all the players stop), or they can be asked to walk like an animal, the teacher rings the bell and everyone freezes, and then a new animal way of walking is introduced.

Relaxation Center-

A relaxation center is a designated area in the home or classroom where children can use comforting strategies. The available relaxation strategies should be specific to the needs of the child or classroom constitution. Relaxation activities can include bean bags or large pillows to relax and cuddle in, squeeze balls, bubbles for blowing, rain sticks, and a relaxation bottle (similar to the angry bottle but combining water, food coloring, glitter, and oil or other slow-moving liquids to create the calming illusion of floating or aerial suspension).

Slow Motion Tag-

In slow motion tag, the therapist or caregiver engages the child in a game of tag in which all participants must move in slow motion.

References

Ainsworth, M. D. S. (1979). Infant-mother attachment. *American Psychologist, 34(10)*, 392–397. doi:10.1037/00003-06x.34.10.932.

Alink, L. R. A., Cicchetti, D., Kim, J., & Rogosch, F. A. (2009). Mediating and moderation process in the relation between maltreatment and psychopathology: Mother-child relationship quality and emotion regulation. *Abnormal Child Psychology, 37(6)*, 831–843. doi:10.1007/s10802-009-9314-4.

Bowlby, J. (1958). The nature of the child's tie to his mother. *International Journal of Psychoanalysis, 39*, 350–373.

Bowlby, J. (1980). *Attachment and loss: Vol. 3. Sadness and depression.* New York: Basic Books.

Brazelton, T. B. (1992). *Touchpoints: Your child's emotional and behavioral development.* Reading, Massachusetts: Perseus Books.

Fonagy, P., Gergely, G., Jurist, E. L., & Target, M. (2004). *Affect regulation mentalization, and the development of the self.* London: Karnac Ltd.

Fraiberg, S., Adelson, E., & Shapiro, V. (1975). Ghosts in the nursery: a psychoanalytic approach to the problems of impaired infant-mother relationships. *Journal of the American Academy of Child Psychiatry, 14*, 387–402.

Freud, A. (1946). *The ego and the mechanisms of defense.* New York: International Universities Press.

Gergely, G., & Watson, J. (1996). The social biofeedback theory of parental affect-mirroring: The development of emotional self-awareness and self-control in infancy. *International Journal of Psycho-Analysis, 77*, 1181–1211.

Greenspan, S. (2007). Six developmental stages. Retrieved from http://www.icdl.com/dirFloortime/overview/SixDevelopmentalMilestones.shtml

Hane, A. A., & Fox, N. A. (2006). Ordinary variations in maternal caregiving influence human infants' stress reactivity. *Psychological Science, 17(6)*, 550–556.

Klein, M. (1932). *The psycho-analysis of children.* London: Hogarth Press. Retrieved from http://www.pep-web.org/document.php?id=ipl.022.0001a&PHPSESSID =qo92 uopitioc6ccioosku2mc30.

Kochanska, G., Philibert, R. A., & Barry, R. A. (2009). Interplay of genes and early mother-child relationship in the development of self-regulation from toddler to preschool age. *Journal of Child Psychology and Psychiatry, 50(11)*, 1331–1338. doi:10.1111/j.1469-7610.2008.02050.x.

Lillas, C., & Turnbull, J. (2009). *Infant/child mental health, early intervention, and relationship-based therapies: A neurorelational framework for interdisciplinary practice.* New York: W.W. Norton & Co., Inc.

Perry, B. (2001). Bonding and attachment in maltreated children: Consequences of emotional neglect in childhood. Retrieved from http://www.childtrauma.org/images/stories/Articles/attcar4_03_v2_r.pdf.

Schore, A. N. (1994). *Affect regulation and the origin of the self: The neurobiology of emotional development.* Mahwah NJ: Erlbaum.

Schore, A. N. (2001). Effects of a secure attachment relationship on right brain development, affect regulation, and infant mental health. *Infant Mental Health Journal, 22(1–2)*, 7–66.

Siegel, D. (1999). *The developing mind: How relationships and the brain interact to shape who we are.* New York: Guilford Press.

Thomas, A., & Chess, S. (1977). *Temperament and development.* Oxford England: Brunner/Mazel.

Werner, E. E., & Smith, R. S. (1992). *Overcoming the odds: High risk children from birth to adulthood.* New York: Cornell University Press.

ZERO TO THREE. (2005). *Diagnostic classification: 0–3R: Diagnostic classification of mental health and developmental disorders of infancy and early childhood* (Rev. ed.). Washington, DC: Zero to Three Press.

About the Author

Dr. Barbara Stroud is a licensed clinical psychologist currently living in California. She is a member of the Academy of ZERO TO THREE Fellows, and is endorsed as an Infant-Family Early Childhood Mental Health Specialist and Reflective Facilitator Mentor (by the **California Center for Infant-Family and Early Childhood Mental Health**). She is also a faculty member at the University of Massachusetts Boston Infant-Parent Program, Napa campus. Dr. Stroud has provided numerous training at the national level. Some of Dr. Stroud's training contacts include: Los Angeles County Department of Mental Health, Santa Clara County First Five, California Child Care Resource and Referral Network, ZERO TO THREE's Military Families Project, WestEd, San Bernardino County, Cal State Long Beach, and Cal State Northridge. Her passion for the needs of vulnerable children and families is evident in her personal and professional work. Throughout her career, Dr. Stroud has endeavored to motivate and improve service delivery models for mental health professionals as well as children and families. Based on this philosophy, **How to Measure a Relationship** has been designed to support and enhance the professional competency of service providers who work with the birth to five population.

Made in the USA
Columbia, SC
03 August 2018